Celebrating your year

1955

a very special year for

A message from the author:

Welcome to the year 1955.

I trust you will enjoy this fascinating romp down memory lane.

And when you have reached the end of the book, please join me in the battle against AI generated copy-cat books and fake reviews.

Details are near the back of the book.

Best regards,
Bernard Bradforsand-Tyler.

Contents

Family Life in 1955 America	9
A Decade of Change for the UK	13
Our Love Affair with Cars	17
Tuning in to Television	23
Most Popular TV Shows of 1955	24
The Long Struggle for Civil Rights	28
Rosa Parks and the Montgomery Bus Boycott	29
The Cold War—Nuclear Arms Race	30
The Cold War—On the Ground and in the Skies	31
McDonalds' National Expansion	34
Einstein Dies at 76	35
Coup d'état Ousts Perón	36
Cinema and Films of 1955	38
Top Grossing Films of 1955	39
James Dean—Death of an Icon	40
Cat on a Hot Tin Roof Opens on Broadway	44
Disneyland's Grand Opening	46
The Lord of the Rings Trilogy	48
First Guinness Book of Records	49
A Rock 'n' Roll Revolution	51
Billboard Top 30 Songs of 1955	52
Fashion Trends of the 1950s	55
A Vaccine for Polio	66
Science and Medicine	67
Other News from 1955	68
Famous People Born in 1955	72
1955 in Numbers	76
Image Attributions	84

Advertisement

PACKAGED PRODUCE HELPS ME SHOP IN A JIFFY

"I never have to wait till a clerk is free! Fruits and vegetables are weighed and priced, packaged in Cellophane... I just pick what I want and go on my way! They're cleaner, too ...ready to pop into the refrigerator, wrapper and all. And many are trimmed to save work and waste."

Shopping's easier: fruits and vegetables are clean and fresh in DuPont Cellophane

Packaged produce helps me shop in a jiffy

"I never have to wait till a clerk is free! Fruits and vegetables ae weighed and priced, packaged in Cellophane...I just pick what I want and go on my way! They're cleaner, too...ready to pop into the refrigerator, wrapper and all. And many are trimmed to save work and waste."

Shopping's easier: fruits and vegetables are clean and fresh in DuPont Cellophane

Let's flashback to 1955, a very special year.

Was this the year you were born?

Was this the year you were married?

Whatever the reason, this book is a celebration of your year,

THE YEAR 1955.

Turn the pages to discover a book packed with fun-filled fabulous facts. We look at the people, the places, the politics and the pleasures that made 1955 unique and helped shape the world we know today.

So get your time-travel suit on, and enjoy this trip down memory lane, to rediscover what life was like, back in the year 1955.

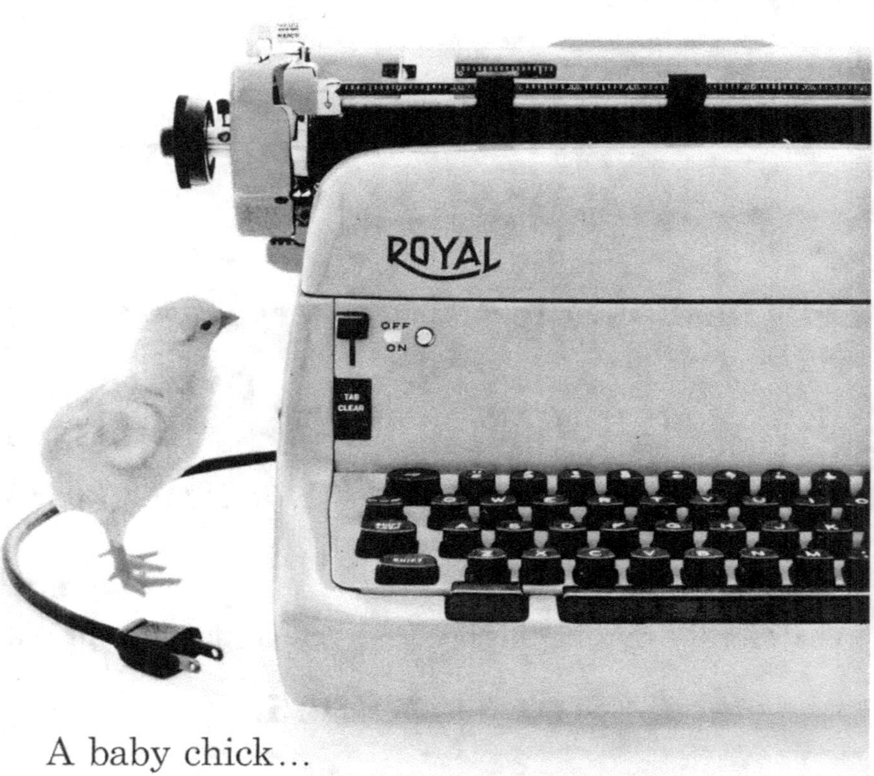

A baby chick...
the new Royal electric and you

Cuddlesome? Cute? And the baby chick weighs only about two ounces.

Did you realize it takes less weight than this to depress one key of the new Royal Electric? When you get to the end of a line, it takes only three ounces to push down the carriage return key.

It's 13 times easier to do these familiar jobs on the new Royal Electric than on a non-electric typewriter. Isn't this a pretty good reason why you need a new Royal Electric?

Besides, you do your usual quota of work with time to spare. Your fingers don't get dog-tired at the end of the day. Your typing looks great, flattering both you and the boss.

Learn about the many other exclusive conveniences of this new kind of electric typewriter in a personal office demonstration. It is designed with you in mind by the world's largest manufacturer of typewriters.

Call your Royal Representative.

ROYAL® electrics *standards • portables • Roytype® business supplies*

The Royal Typewriter Company, Division of Royal McBee Corporation

A baby chick...the new Royal electric and you

Cuddlesome? Cute? And the baby chick weighs only about two ounces.

Did you realize it takes less weight than this to depress one key of the new Royal Electric? When you get to the end of a line, it takes only three ounces to push down the carriage return key.

It's 13 times easier to do these familiar jobs on the new Royal Electric than on a non-electric typewriter. Isn't this a pretty good reason why you need a new Royal Electric?

Besides, you do you usual quota of work with time to spare. Your fingers don't get dog-tired at the end of the day. Your typing looks great, flattering both you and the boss.

Learn about the many other exclusive conveniences of this new kind of electric typewriter in a personal office demonstration. It is designed with you in mind by the world's largest manufacturer of typewriters. Call your Royal Representative.

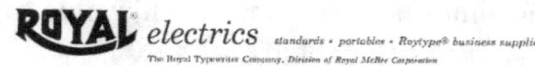

Family Life in 1955 America

Imagine if time-travel was a reality, and one fine morning you wake up to find yourself flashed back in time, back to the year 1955.

What would life be like for a typical family, in a typical town, somewhere in America?

A typical family in 1955.

The post-war boom delivered us a booming economy, booming birth numbers, booming suburbs, and the booming trappings of the consumerist culture we still live in today.

Our rising middle classes were feeling an pressing need to spend, with consumer demand for everything innovative, bigger, or better, reaching new highs year after year.

In the year 1955 there were 4.05 million babies born (up from 2.8 million at the end of the war ten years earlier).[1]

Massive suburban developments, built on the outskirts of towns, catered to our increased demand for family homes. Sales were boosted by returned soldiers who had access to low interest loans through the G.I. Bill of 1944.

From 1952-1958, 17,300 homes were built in the massive suburban development of Levittown, Pennsylvania.

Our middle-class desire for everything new and modern, which we just loved to show-off, kept businesses profitable and production on the increase. With only 6% of the world's population in 1955, the USA was producing almost half the world's goods.

An energetic advertising industry, through TV, radio and print, ensured we always knew what our next purchase could and should be.

[1] U.S Census Bureau Statistical Abstract of the United States: 1960, page 52
[2] ageofaffluence.weebly.com.

Joining the television in our families' list of must-haves were: defrost refrigerators, front-loading dryers, fully-automatic washing machines, vacuum cleaners, air-conditioning and heating units, milkshake makers, and a multitude of other kitchen gadgets and home appliances. In addition we needed a family car, motorcycle, bicycles, hiking and camping gear, picnic set, and much, much more.

New! G·E automatic cooking unit
You just "set it and forget it"

The average family income was $4,400 a year.[1] Unemployment was 4.2% and falling, with GDP growth at 7.1%.[2]

Average costs in 1955 [3]	
New house	$18,346
New car	$1,900
Television	$100
A gallon of gasoline	$0.29

But beneath the appearance of domestic bliss, Americans were deeply concerned. The threat of the Soviet Union (USSR) was ever present. The Cold War dominated US policies and communist fears gripped the nation throughout the decade and beyond.

By the end of 1955, both the US and USSR had successfully developed and detonated hydrogen bombs. The nuclear arms race was well underway. We would endure another 36 years of tension between the two super-powers before the Cold War finally ended with the dissolution of the Soviet Union in 1991.

[1] census.gov/library/publications/1957/demo/p60-024.html.
[2] thebalance.com/unemployment-rate-by-year-3305506.
[3] thepeoplehistory.com.

Advertisement

These are the finest of the new Maytag washers and dryers. See the complete line of wringer and automatic washers, dryers, ironers, ranges and freezers...all made by Maytag.

new Maytag can save 9 gallons of <u>hot</u> water per load!

It's completely automatic, even for small loads!
Save 11½ gallons of water every time you wash a small load – and 9 gallons of this is *hot* water! Think of the savings over the years. Exclusive new Automatic Water Level Control saves on *both* wash and rinse, uses only the water you need for any size load. On full loads the Maytag Automatic uses less water than any other agitator type automatic—as much as 50% less. Exclusive Gyrafoam action and Double-Spin Tubs wash the grimiest work clothes —the most delicate fabrics—thoroughly clean. Matching gas or electric dryer. Ask your dealer how *easy* it is to own a Maytag. The Maytag Company, Newton, Iowa.

AUTOMATIC WATER LEVEL CONTROL— Saves up to 11½ gallons of water on small loads—9 gallons are hot water!

FASTEST SAFETY BRAKE—Maytag Safety Lid stops action the *moment* it's opened. Sure protection for your youngsters.

MAYTAG ADVANCED AUTOMATICS

It's <u>completely</u> automatic, even for small loads!

Save $11^1/_2$ gallons of water every time you wash a small load—and 9 gallons of this is *hot* water! Think of the savings over the years. Exclusive new Automatic Water Level Control saves on *both* wash and rinse, uses only the water you need for any size load! On full loads the Maytag Automatic uses less water than any other agitator type automatic—as much as 50% less. Exclusive Gyrafoam action and Double-Spin Tubs wash the grimiest work clothes—the most delicate fabrics—thoroughly clean. Matching gas or electric dryer. Ask your dealer how *easy* it is to own a Maytag. *The Maytag Company, Newton, Iowa.*

Fastest safety brake—Maytag Safety Lid stops action the moment it's opened. Sure protection for your youngsters.

A Decade of Change for the United Kingdom

Now just imagine you flashed back to a town in 1955 United Kingdom or Western Europe.

Unlike boom-time America, a very different picture would await you.

Many major cities like London bore the brunt of destruction from WWII bombings. The post-war rebuilding process required major loans from the USA and other nations, leaving the UK deep in long-term debt. With austerity measures on everything from fabrics to food, the British were forced to tighten their collective belts,

A central London street in 1955.

With the last of the post-war austerity restrictions ending in 1954, the British populace was feeling the positive winds of change. Job security and record low unemployment saw the middle and working classes feeling prosperous and optimistic. Living standards were rising and families had money to spend.

Advertisement

How many ways can you use a camera like this?

It's the most compact all-purpose snapshot camera ever made. It's an outdoor-indoor camera It's a daytime nighttime camera It's a black-and-white camera and a color camera, too.

It's small enough to carry with you anywhere. Yet you get standard enlarged prints the size of a postcard (3½" x 5") ... full-color snaps, too, with Kodacolor Film.

It's a well-engineered, handsomely styled little picture-maker, soundly constructed for years of service.

It's so easy to use, it's the ideal "first camera" for beginners, young or old. There are no settings to make. The lens is prefocused for you at the factory. All you do is aim and shoot.

It's inexpensive to operate. It uses thrifty No. 127 film—8 snaps to a roll.

It's priced so low ($4.95 including Federal Tax, Flasholder $3.20) you can afford more than one—for each of the youngsters, for instance. You can even have one just to keep in the baby's room, loaded and ready at all times, so you won't miss a single fleeting mood or expression.

It's the handiest, most compact flash camera that Kodak ingenuity has yet devised.

It's the Brownie Holiday Flash Camera—and whether you want one for yourself or for a gift, it's well worth a visit to your nearest Kodak dealer.

Camera and Flasholder shown actual size

Eastman Kodak Company, Rochester 4, N. Y.

Kodak

How many ways can you use a camera like this? It's the most compact all-purpose snapshot camera ever made. It's an outdoor-indoor camera. It's a daytime nighttime camera. It's a black-and-white camera and a color camera too.

It's small enough to carry with you anywhere. Yet you get standard enlarged prints the size of a postcard ($3^1/_2$" x 5")...full-color snaps, too, with Kodacolor Film. It's a well-engineered, handsomely styled little picture-maker, soundly constructed for years of service. It's so easy to use, it's the ideal "first camera" for beginners, young or old. There are no settings to make. The lens is prefocussed for you at the factory. All you do is aim and shoot. Its inexpensive to operate. It uses thrifty No. 127 film–8 snaps to a roll. It's priced so low ($4.95, Flasholder $320) you can afford more than one–for each of the youngsters for instance. You can even have one just to keep in the baby's room, loaded and ready at all times, so you won't miss a single fleeting mood or expression. It's the handiest, most compact flash camera that Kodak ingenuity has yet devised

It's the Brownie Holiday Flash Camera–and whether you want one for yourself or for a gift, it's well worth a visit to your nearest Kodak dealer.

Young adults in particular had spare cash to burn on leisure and luxuries. Even teenagers had money to spend. Looking for a new voice, the British youth of the mid-'50s turned to American rock 'n' roll music and fashion, giving rise to a distinct youth culture focused on freedom and rebellion.

British teenagers at a party.

Internationally, lack of excess finance made it increasingly difficult for Great Britain to continue financing and keeping secure its far-flung colonies. As a result, many British colonies would be released during the following ten years, gaining independence as new nations. The United Kingdom was losing its super-power status on the world's stage.

Advertisement

The *New* PACKARD

WITH TORSION-LEVEL RIDE

THE NEW PACKARD "FOUR HUNDRED"—"ASK THE MAN WHO OWNS ONE"

Greatest Ride Development in Automotive History

The New Packard with Torsion-Level Ride
Greatest Ride Development in Automotive History

Pride of possession–a gleam in the owner's eye...ardent admiration–a gleam in *other* eyes...this is the impression the *new* Packard is making on owner and onlooker, alike!

Packard engineers, in common with Packard designers, had exclusiveness as their objective. For *only* Packard has Torsion-Level Ride which eliminates coil and leaf springs...smooths the road...levels the load–*automatically!* In other cars the twisting forces of wheel shock are sent to the frame, creating pitch and bounce and wracking of the frame and body. In Packard, these same forces are transmitted along the new suspension system and absorbed *before* they reach frame or passengers. And an ingenious power-controlled levelizer keeps the *new* Packard always at "flight-level" regardless of load.

Packard owners can be proud of more than the ride. A new "free-breathing" V-8 engine. 275 horsepower in the Caribbean, 260 in all other models, delivers more driving force to the rear wheels, at all road speeds, than any other American passenger car engine. And new Packard Twin Ultramatic is the smoothest, most alert of all automatic transmissions.

Gracefully contoured and luxuriously appointed, here is the *one* new car in the fine car field. Your Packard dealer will be happy to place the keys to a *new* Packard at your disposal...drive it an *let the ride decide!*

Our Love Affair with Cars

By 1955, the US dominated the world's car market, producing more than half of all new vehicles internationally. In just ten years, the car industry had shifted from fabricating utilitarian war tanks and trucks, to producing fashionable consumer vehicles, the kind of which we just had to have.

There were now 52 million registered cars on US roads, up from 25.7 million ten years earlier.[1] Rising incomes meant the car was no longer considered a luxury reserved only for the wealthy. Our love affair with cars had begun.

General Motors rolls out the cars at its new engine plant in Flint, MI.

Teenagers at a drive-through in the mid-'50s.

Services related business such as drive-through restaurants and drive-in cinemas were springing up everywhere, especially popular among the younger generation.

[1] fhwa.dot.gov/ohim/summary95/mv200.pdf.

Our love affair with cars grew hand-in-hand with the post-war baby boom and housing construction boom. Where would we be without our cars? How else could we get from our far-flung suburban homes to our downtown offices?

Car manufacturers competed for our attention with stylish designs, larger engines, and added detailing. The rising middle classes had money to spend, and cars became the ultimate status symbol.

Cars were no longer just a necessity; they had become an expression of our personality. Sturdy, sporty, powerful or luxurious, cars now came in a wide range of styles, colors, and price-points. Decorative chrome and tail fins reached new heights as the decade progressed, adorned with wings and stripes for added pizzazz.

Advertisement

First it warms your heart... (That Thunderbird styling!)
Then it reads your mind... (That Trigger-Torque Power!)

It's amazing how just *looking* at the '55 Ford gives so many people that wonderful feeling. Why not? There's "Thunderbird" written in almost every line... from the hooded headlights to the flat rear deck. Inside, you'll see new exciting color harmonies in durable fabrics. All in all, there isn't a more *pleasing* car in sight.

Behind the wheel of the new Ford, *you* become a new man. For under your foot lies response so eager and alive, you almost believe it's clairvoyant! This is Ford's Trigger-Torque power... and it replies to your driving demands with split-second agility. There's safety in power like this... to whizz you out of traffic snarls... and to pass you ahead when passing is called for. Three new stout-hearted engines to choose from. And at least a score of other new engineering features. Reading about it is nowhere near the fun of driving the new Ford. So why not visit your dealer today?

Advertisement

"Guests of Honor" Wherever They Go!

YOUR CADILLAC DEALER

"Guests of Honor" Wherever They Go!

Not long after a motorist takes delivery of his first Cadillac car, he makes a truly wonderful and thrilling discovery.

No matter where he travels at the wheel of his Cadillac, he finds that he is accorded an extra measure of courtesy and respect.

And this discovery will be all the more rewarding for the man or woman who makes the move to Cadillac in 1955. For the "car of cars" now offers more of everything to inspire the respect and admiration of people everywhere.

Its world-famous beauty, for example, is more majestic and distinctive than ever before. Its celebrated interior luxury and elegance are far more wonderful to behold... and to enjoy. And its performance is, from every standpoint, the finest in Cadillac history!

If you haven't as yet taken the time for a personal inspection and demonstration of the 1955 Cadillac—you ought to come in soon and do so.

You'll be a most welcome guest—at any time!

Five car-producing countries dominated the industry by the start of 1955: England, France, Germany and Italy, with America in the top spot. (Japan had yet to enter this elite group.)

Top: MGA by MG, 1955-'56.
Left: SAAB 93, 1955.
Below: Pegaso Z-103, 1955.

US car manufacturers produced 8 million vehicles in 1955 alone, accounting for more than 90% of cars sold in the country.

Detroit was America's car manufacturing powerhouse, where "the Big Three" (General Motors, Ford and Chrysler) produced year-on-year bigger, longer and heavier gas-guzzlers to satisfy the '50s consumer desire for power and style over efficiency and safety.

Detroit had become the fifth largest city in the US, and by the end of the decade, a whopping one in six American adults would be employed in the car industry nation-wide.[1]

In 1955, General Motors sold more than all its competitors combined, becoming the first US company to generate more than $1 billion in sales.[2]

GM Chevrolet assembly line, 1955.

[1] theweek.com/articles/461968/rise-fall-detroit-timeline.
[2] ageofaffluence.weebly.com.

Advertisement

BIGGER-THAN-LIFE! THAT'S THE GIANT PICTURE YOU GET WITH THE NEW 24-INCH "BAYLOR". EBONY FINISH. MODEL 24S512. $299.95.

The big new television thrill from RCA Victor—

BIGGER-THAN-LIFE 24-INCH TV WITH THE "ALL-CLEAR" PICTURE

Top value—peak performance—at every price level—$149.95 to $500

The big new television thrill from RCA Victor–
Bigger-than-life 24-inch TV with the "all-clear" picture

TV entertainment has come of age... with today's bigger, more spectacular programs. But you miss half the fun of a king-size show when it's squeezed into a small-size screen.

That's why the new and beautiful RCA Victor 24-inch table models make such happy news. For only $299.95—less than you might pay for many a smaller-screen set—you can now have a picture that's actually bigger-than-life!

What's more, RCA Victor TV sets are the only ones with the famous "All-Clear" Picture–and that's all-important with 24-inch TV. You see, as the picture grows bigger, fine picture quality becomes increasingly necessary. The RCA Victor "All-Clear" Picture–with 212% greater contrast–is TV's finest and clearest. It's another RCA Victor exclusive!

All RCA Victor 24-inch sets also have such advances as "Golden Throat" Fidelity Sound... "Magic Monitor" chassis for finest reception possible... new light-up tuning. See the great variety of handsome RCA Victor table models and consoles now on display at your RCA Victor dealer's. See for yourself why every year more people buy RCA Victor than any other television.

Top value—peak performance—at every price level—$149 to $500

Tuning in to Television

By 1955, 64% of US households owned a television set.[1] Television had firmly become the preferred means of entertainment for our rising middle classes.

Typical family watching television in the '50s.

The early '50s would become known as the first "Golden Age of Television". During this time, live TV broadcasts from New York City dominated, based on radio and the theatrical traditions of Broadway.

However by 1955, the newer formats produced out of Los Angeles were gaining in popularity—sitcoms, soap operas, westerns, quiz shows, crime and medical dramas would soon become our primetime staples.

Natalie Wood and Gig Young in *Warner Brothers Presents* (ABC. 1955-1956).

The big Hollywood film studios, who had until now frowned upon television, had finally accepted that TV was here to stay, and they sought profitable ways to enter the small-screen business.

In 1955, Warner Brothers, MGM and 20th Century Fox aired their first made-for-TV shows. Over the next five years these Hollywood produced programs would succeed in dominating TV primetime.

[1] americancentury.omeka.wlu.edu/items/show/136.

Most Popular TV Shows of 1955

1	The $64,000 Question	11	General Electric Theater
2	I Love Lucy	12	Private Secretary
3	The Ed Sullivan Show	=	Ford Theater
4	Disneyland	14	The Red Skelton Show
5	The Jack Benny Show	15	The George Gobel Show
6	December Bride	16	Arthur Godfrey's Talent Scouts
7	You Bet Your Life	17	The Lineup
8	Dragnet	18	The Perry Como Show
9	The Millionaire	19	The Honeymooners
10	I've Got a Secret	20	The Adventures of Robin Hood

* From the Nielsen Media Research 1955-'56 season of top-rated primetime TV series in the USA.

The $64,000 Question captured the nation's attention from the moment it debuted in June 1955, till its sudden demise 3 years later. The show was canceled following the scandalous exposure of game show rigging, where questions and answers were provided to preferred contestants prior to filming. (CBS. 1955-1958).

Ronald Reagan, as host and part owner of *General Electric Theater*, became known as "The Great Communicator". It is said he developed his public-speaking skills through the many public forums he was invited to speak at. (CBS. 1953-1962).

Angie Dickinson and James Craig in *The Millionaire* (CBS. 1955-1960).

The original Mouseketeers of *The Mickey Mouse Club* (ABC. 1955-'59).

The television networks were quick to turn out new programs to keep us tuning in. Here are just a few of the new programs that aired for the first time in 1955: *The Millionaire, The Mickey Mouse Club, The Benny Hill Show* (UK), and *The Adventures of Robin Hood (UK)*. Other notables include *The $64,000 Question, The Perry Como Show, The Honeymooners, This is Your Life* (UK) and the hugely popular *Gunsmoke*, which aired for 20 seasons.

James Arness, Amanda Blake, Milburn Stone, & Dennis Weaver in *Gunsmoke* (CBS. 1955-1975).

Alexander Gauge & Richard Greene in *The Adventures of Robin Hood* (ITV. 1955-1959).

Advertisement

Your family deserves the finest television—Magnavox!

Television is so important to your family that it is folly to buy any but the finest. And Magnavox—the finest—costs no more—priced as low as $149.50. Magnavox, leader in style and quality, again sets a new standard of beauty, performance and value that are years ahead of the industry. You have the widest choice of fine instruments—furniture designs to fit every décor. See the dramatic new values shown here and many more at your Magnavox dealer's. His name is listed under "Television" in the classified telephone book.

1. The Magnarama 24—newest big-screen television. The set of tomorrow with 100sq.in. more picture in a cabinet no larger than average 21-inch table size. Concealed top controls, 2-speaker front-projected sound, aluminized tube. Including stand, $249.50.
2. The Video Theatre 21-in. TV with 12-in. and 5-in. speakers. New top-tuning concealed controls. Genuine mahogany, limed oak, and cherry. In mahogany, $279.50.
3. The Magnasonic 210—gives you a true high-fidelity phonograph in a console priced no more than a good table model....only $149.50.
4. The Telerama 21—beautiful new compact television receiver encased in genuine hand-rubbed mahogany cabinet...Complete with stand, $239.50.

Advertisement

The new Underwood 150 is the typewriter designed to keep your hands lovely to look at.

Two important improvements make the new Underwood 150 the typewriter most wanted by the girls who make business hum. Underwood has always been designed with the user in mind. That's why it's so good looking and has so many extra features to make turning out crisp, clean work practically automatic. Now, look how Underwood and Underwood alone helps you keep fingernails and hands lovely to look at, lovely to touch!

Exclusive half-moon keys: formed to fit fingers. Half-moon tops mean fingernails never touch the keys. No more worrying about short unfashionable fingernails, chipped nail polish! Exclusive touch tuning: Stubborn typewriter keys often give girls rough, widened fingertips. Underwood's touch is kitten-soft. 28 easy-to-set touch variations! You choose touch to suit finger-tips, always look fresh from the manicurist!

The Long Struggle for Civil Rights

The mid-'50s saw a new chapter in America's Civil Rights Movement being launched. Activism shifted from political lobbying to non-violent direct action. Lasting from 1954 to 1968, this new focus saw sit-ins, boycotts, marches, protests, freedom rides, and acts of civil disobedience become hallmarks of the Movement.

17th May 1954—The US Supreme Court ruled in the case of Brown vs. Board of Education, that state based racial segregation in public schools was unconstitutional. This was a major victory for civil rights activists, instigating a new chapter in the Civil Rights Movement.

Lawyers George E.C. Hayes, Thurgood Marshall, and James M. Nabrit, Jr., celebrating outside the US Supreme Court, Washington, D.C., 17th May '54.

28th Aug 1955—14-year-old African American Emmett Till, was brutally murdered for allegedly flirting with a white woman. He was beaten close to death before being thrown into Mississippi's Tallahatchie River, tied to a heavy object with barbed wire.

The perpetrators were found "not guilty" by an all-white jury, sparking a call-to-action against racial violence and injustice. A generation of African Americans were galvanized to join the Civil Rights Movement.

Newspapers across the country highlighted the reality and injustice of race relations in the South.

5th Dec 1955—Black commuters of Montgomery, Alabama, staged a one day boycott of the city's busses. Turning into a long-term boycott, this is regarded as the first large scale civil rights protest in the USA.

Rosa Parks and the Montgomery Bus Boycott

42-year-old civil rights activist Rosa Parks was arrested on a Montgomery bus on 1st Dec 1955, for refusing to give up her seat to a white passenger.

During Park's trial 4 days later, 500 supporters came to the court-house, while a further 40,000 commuters boycotted the buses, car pooling or walking to work.

Dr. Martin Luther King Jr., then a young pastor at a local Baptist Church, lead the Bus Boycott. Through his captivating and inspiring speeches, King was soon catapulted up the ranks of the Civil Rights Movement.

The Montgomery Bus Boycott lasted 381 days until a U.S. Supreme Court ruling declared segregation on public transport to be unconstitutional.

The No. 2857 bus on which Parks was riding before her arrest, exhibited at the Henry Ford Museum in Detroit MI. Statues of Parks' sitting on a bus at the National Civil Rights Museum in Memphis TN, and in the United States Capitol.

From top: Rosa Parks with Dr. Martin Luther King jr. 1955.
Riding a bus, 1956.
Being fingerprinted by police, '56.

Parks continued fighting for equality throughout her long and prolific life.

When she died on the 24th October 2005, she became the first woman, and only second African American, to lie in honor in the US State Rotunda.

The Cold War–Nuclear Arms Race

Cold War tensions between the two former allies–the USSR and the USA–continued from post war 1945 till 1991.

Starting in the USA as policies for communist containment, the distrust and misunderstanding between the two sides quickly escalated from political squabbling to a military nuclear arms race. Trillions of dollars in military spending saw both sides stockpile their nuclear arsenals, strategically pointing and positioning their missiles closer and closer to each other.

The superpowers also raced to develop more powerful bombs and longer reaching missiles. The USA tested its first hydrogen bomb in 1952, with the USSR testing theirs in November 1955.

In January 1955, the US Airforce awarded Convair a contract to develop a long range intercontinental ballistic missile, capable of delivering a nuclear weapon. Two years later the Soviets would confirm they had long range missiles able to reach any corner of the earth.

USA ballistic missile ready to launch, 1955.

By 1955, the USA had a stockpile of 2422 nuclear weapons, against the Soviet's 200 weapons.[1] Both sides continued to increase their stockpiles. American stockpiles peaked in 1966 with a total of 31,175 against the Soviet's 7,089 weapons.[1]

The USSR continued to grow their stockpile until 1988. In 1991, the Nuclear Arms Race ended with the signing of a denuclearization treaty.

[1] tandfonline.com/doi/pdf/10.2968/066004008.

The Cold War–On the Ground and in the Skies

14th May– The Soviet Union and seven Eastern Bloc allies signed *The Warsaw Pact*, cementing the communist military and political alliance as a counter to NATO.

Fearful that a "domino effect" would see an uncontained spread of communism across the world, the 1950s saw America embroiled in two major Southeast Asian wars–the Korean War (1950-1953) and the Vietnam War (1955-1973).

On the 1st November 1955, US personnel of the Military Assistance Advisory Group were deployed to train the South Vietnamese Army. This would mark the start of US involvement in the Vietnamese war.

The US committed to supporting South Vietnam, financially and militarily, during its 30-year-long bloody civil war against North Vietnam (the Viet Cong). At the same time, communist China and USSR were jointly aiding the Viet Cong's invasion southward. Vietnam had become a Cold War battlefield.

The Cold War turned skywards on 29th July 1955, when the USA announced its intent to launch an artificial satellite. Four days later, on 2nd August, the Soviets announced their intention to do the same "in the near future." Space would become the next battlefield for superpower superiority. The Space Race, which was to dominate most of the 1960s, was underway.

The Man in the $70,000 hat

He's Navy... every inch. A flier in the New Air Navy. Young... dedicated... serious. A man whose business is the active defense of every American. Maybe you know him. He comes from the house next door... or the farm down the road. Yesterday he delivered your newspaper, or lent a hand at harvest time. Today he's flying jets from a Navy carrier. He's a proud man... and he has a right to be. Not everybody can be a Navy flier. Not everybody can graduate to wear glistening wings of gold and the stripes of a Navy ensign.

Training is thorough... painstaking and unforgettable. It's executive training that will stand him in good stead all his life. Private money can't buy it. But the Navy gives it to those who qualify. It costs about $70,000 to build a Navy flier... and when a man graduates... he's ready to wear that $70,000 hat.

He's equipped to man the newest Navy jets. He's learned to live by Navy's strict code of safety... both in aircraft and on the ground. He's an Air Navy man... and America is proud of him. America needs more men like him now! Men who can carry responsibility... who want to take their place in the new jet age. Men who want to take hold of their future and give it direction. Men who can wear a $70,000 hat. Men like yourself, perhaps?

Advertisement

British Vintage Airline Posters from 1955.

McDonalds' National Expansion   15th April 1955

What is it about McDonalds that makes the fast-food giant so extraordinary? It remains one of the world's most loved fast-food chains, with almost 40,000 restaurants in more than 100 countries. But it all started back in 1955, with the vision of one man—Ray Kroc.

In 1948, brothers Dick and Mac McDonald opened their first self-service restaurant in San Bernardino, California.

By eliminating waiters, focusing on a minimal, highly profitable burger-focussed menu, and developing assembly-line food systems, the brothers "invented" the notion of fast-food.

Dick and Mac McDonalds' first burger restaurant in San Bernardino, 1948.

Ray Kroc's first McDonalds franchise opened in Illinois, Chicago on 15th April 1955.

Enter Ray Kroc, seller of milkshake machines. Kroc had come to see why McDonalds had purchased so many of his machines. Impressed by their operations, Kroc convinced the brothers to give him nation-wide franchise rights.

In return for half a percent of gross sales, Kroc would seek funding, set up the franchisees, and absorb all risks. Business savvy Kroc separately set up another company, to buy the land and build the restaurants that all franchisees would be required to lease.

To gain total control, Kroc bought out the McDonald brothers' share in 1961 for $2.7 million, and the rest, as they say, is history.

Einstein Dies at 76

18th April 1955

18th April– Albert Einstein passed away at Princeton Hospital, NJ. The German-born theoretical physicist had been admitted one day earlier with internal bleeding accompanied by severe pain, caused by a burst abdominal aortic aneurysm. He was 76 years old.

Regarded as one of the most brilliant minds of the modern era, Einstein was most famous for developing the theory of relativity, and for the mass-energy formula $E=mc^2$.

In 1921 he was awarded the Nobel Prize in Physics for his discovery of the law of the photoelectric effect.

Helen Dukas, Einstein's long-time secretary and companion, recounted him saying: "You're really hysterical—I have to pass on sometime, and it doesn't really matter when." Einstein died peacefully the next morning.

Coup d'état Ousts Perón

16th September 1955

16th September– Argentinian President Juan Domingo Perón was ousted following a violent coup, resulting in a military dictatorship for Argentina, and exile for Perón. He would return to Argentina in 1973, winning the presidency again later that year.

Populist Perón began his first presidency in 1946, winning with promises of social justice and economic independence.

He is remembered for his record investments in health care, public works and housing construction. And for his efforts to stimulate industrial growth, increase workers' pay, and reduce poverty and unemployment. His political ideals were neither capitalist nor socialist, but a unique blend of nationalism and populism known as Perónism, a movement which continues to this day.

Although being extremely popular, Perón was intolerant of opposition, resorting to violence and fascist rule to maintain control. He was opposed by the middle classes, intelligentsia, and the church.

In 1955, controversial new reforms to legalize divorce and prostitution spurred his opposers to take action.

Following a bomb attack killing 364 supporters, Perónists retaliated by burning several churches.

Perón is also remembered for his beautiful second wife, Eva, who was adored by the people for her political activities on behalf of women, the poor and the working-class.

Advertisement

New...The Aristocrat...in the treasured 1955 World Book series

Only World Book deserves to be encased in the new Aristocrat binding, classic example of the bookbinder's art. The distinctive agelessness of ivory, the unquestioned richness of 24K gold make the Aristocrat Edition a modern heirloom for your family. Merely touch the covers and you have an invitation to the world of wonders within.

World Book spans the breadth of man's knowledge from prehistoric periods through the atomic future. It's a priceless collection of tens of thousands of interesting facts to enrich and enlarge your family's background. Yet, with all its beauty, the Aristocrat Edition is not destined to be a lock-and-key showpiece. World Book is created to be used. So naturally, the handsome heritage covers are both durable and washable. It's superb in every respect.

Wouldn't you be proud to have it in your home?

The Aristocrat Binding $169–$10 down, $10 a month.
The President Red Binding $129–$10 down, $6 a month.

1st in sales!
More people buy World Book than any other encyclopedia

Cinema and Films of 1955

Kim Novak & James Stewart in *Vertigo* (Paramount Pictures, 1958).

With television becoming ever more commonplace in American homes, cinema attendance faced a steady decline throughout the 1950s. In order to win over new audiences, the motion picture industry sought the attention of younger viewers who had more leisure time and cash to spare.

The early to mid-'50s brought a new wave of exciting, young, sexy, anti-hero stars, such as Marlon Brando, James Dean, Kim Novak, Marilyn Monroe and Paul Newman.

Highest Paid Stars

1. James Stewart
2. Grace Kelly
3. John Wayne
4. William Holden
5. Gary Cooper
6. Marilyn Monroe
7. Dean Martin & Jerry Lewis
8. Marlon Brando
9. Humphrey Bogart
10. Clark Gable

Clint Eastwood in 1955.

Paul Newman in 1954.

1955 film debuts

Clint Eastwood	Revenge of the Creature
Shirley MacLaine	The Trouble with Harry
Jayne Mansfield	Female Jungle
Walter Matthau	The Kentuckian
Shirley Jones	Oklahoma!
Joanne Woodward	Count Three and Pray

* From en.wikipedia.org/wiki/1955_in_film.

Top Grossing Films of 1955

1	Cinerama Holiday	Cinerama Production	$10,000,000
2	Mister Roberts	Warner Bros.	$8,500,000
3	Battle Cry	Warner Bros.	$8,100,000
4	Oklahoma!	RKO	$7,100,000
5	Guys and Dolls	MGM	$6,801,000
6	Lady and the Tramp	Disney	$6,500,000
7	Picnic	Columbia	$6,300,000
8	Not as a Stranger	United Artists	$6,200,000
9	Strategic Air Command	Paramount	$6,000,000
=	The Seven Year Itch	20th Century Fox	$6,000,000
=	The Sea Chase	Warner Bros.	$6,000,000
=	To Hell and Back	Universal Pictures	$6,000,000
10	I'll Cry Tomorrow	MGM	$5,873,000

* From en.wikipedia.org/wiki/1955_in_film by box office gross in the USA.

Marilyn Monroe's 23rd film, *The Seven Year Itch*, is most notably remembered for her white dress billowing over a New York subway grate scene.

Disney's 15th animated feature film, *Lady and the Tramp*, was their first to be filmed in new widescreen Cinemascope.

James Dean–Death of an Icon   30th September 1955

Actor James Dean was killed in a head-on collision in Cholame, California, at 4:45pm on 30th September 1955.

His death was announced the next day in newspapers, radio and TV, sending shock waves across the country and catapulting the rising young star to cult status. He remains forever frozen as a symbol of teenage angst. He was only 24 years old.

Remains of Dean's Porche 550 Spyder after the crash.

James Dean in his brand new Porche.

Dean was driving his new Porsche 550 Spyder convertible to Salinas, California, to indulge in his passion for car racing.

Unable to race during filming, Dean was quick to enter the 1st October Salinas Road Race event as soon as filming on his third movie was completed. The collision occurred at an intersection with a left-turning truck. The truck driver and Dean's driving companion both survived the crash. Dean died instantly from a broken neck.

During Dean's short but brilliant acting career he starred in only three major Hollywood films.

In his first film, *East of Eden* (Warner Bros. 1955), Dean portrayed the role of a troubled young teen. Improvising many of the unscripted, deeply emotional scenes, he would be posthumously nominated for an Academy Award the following year.

Dean's second film, *Rebel Without a Cause* (Warner Bros. 1955), would secure his iconic status in American youth culture. As high-school misfit Jim Stark, Dean gave young viewers a hero they could relate to.

Dean starred alongside Rock Hudson and Elizabeth Taylor in his third film, *Giant* (Warner Bros. 1956). Released after his death, the film would earn Dean his second posthumous Academy Award nomination.

Advertisement

Shortest Distance Between 2 Points

New speed to shorten the distance
Quiet luxury to make the time fly

Largest Roomiest Airliner in the World • Far Quieter for Greater Comfort • Wider Aisles • Larger Windows • Wider Seats • Finest Air Conditioning • Restful 5-Cabin Privacy • Congenial Starlight Lounge • Interior Design by Henry Dreyfuss • The Fastest Constellation Ever Built

For all the speed, and quiet comfort, too, fly Super Constellations over every ocean and continent on these 19 leading airlines: Air France • Air India International • Avianca • Cubana • Deutsche Lufthansa • Eastern Air Lines • Iberia • KLM • LAV • Northwest Orient Airlines • Pakistan International • Qantas • Seaboard & Western • Slice Airways • TAP • Thai Airways • Trans-Canada Air Lines • TWA-Trans World Airlines • Varig

Lockheed Super Constellation   Look to Lockheed for Leadership

Advertisement

At last—the thrill of fine stereo at a moderate price
New Kodak Stereo Camera only $84.50

Kodak's new stereo camera is quality through and through, yet costs about half of what you'd expect to have to pay.

What's more, you'll find yourself making excellent 3-dimensional shots with your very first roll. Kodak designers have simplified controls to an astonishing degree. Actually, stereo pictures with the Kodak Stereo Camera are as easy to take as ordinary snapshots. Brilliant f/3.5 lenses, shutter speeds to 1/200, many automatic features—all for a modest $84.50, including Federal Tax.

And 2 superb new viewers with handy focusing controls and adjustable eyepieces. Kodaslide Stereo Viewer I, battery-operated, $12.75. Kodaslide Stereo Viewer II plugs into house circuit, has exclusive brightness control—$23.75. Most Kodak dealers offer convenient terms.

Prices subject to change without notice

Eastman Kodak Company, Rochester 4, N. Y.

Kodak

At last—the thrill of fine stereo at a moderate price
New Kodak Stereo Camera   only $84.50

Kodak's new stereo camera is quality through and through, yet costs about half of what you'd expect to have to pay.

What's more, you'll find yourself making excellent 3-dimensional shots with your very first roll. Kodak designers have simplified controls to an astonishing degree. Actually, stereo pictures with the Kodak Stereo Camera are as easy to take as ordinary snapshots. Brilliant f/3.5 lenses, shutter speeds to 1/200, many automatic features—all for a modest $84.50, including Federal Tax.

And 2 superb new viewers with handy focusing controls and adjustable eyepieces. Kodaslide Stereo Viewer I, battery-operated, $12.75. Kodaslide Stereo Viewer II plugs into house circuit, has exclusive brightness control—$23.75. Most Kodak dealers offer convenient terms.

Cat on a Hot Tin Roof Opens on Broadway

Broadway classic *Cat on a Hot Tin Roof*, based on the Pulitzer Prize-winning book by Tennessee Williams, premiered on 24th March 1955 at the Morosco Theater in New York City. The same year it would receive four Tony nominations and win the Best Drama awards at the Pulitzer Prize and the New York Drama Critics' Circle.

The three-act play opened in London in 1958 and has since seen several Broadway and international revivals.

Theatrical poster from 1955.

Above left: Barbara Bel Geddes and Ben Gazzara in the original Broadway cast, *Cat on a Hot Tin Roof*, 1955.

Above right: Elizabeth Taylor and Paul Newman in the 1958 film.

The 1958 movie version would star Elizabeth Taylor and Paul Newman, two of Hollywood's biggest names, in the leading roles. Most of the book's homosexual themes were removed for the film, which greatly angered Williams.

Cinema poster from 1958 (MGM).

There'll be plenty of action this weekend...
...and you can get it all with your Brownie Movie Camera   only $37.50

Thousands say this is the simplest, surest personal movie camera ever made. With it, folks everywhere are already enjoying family movies.

The Brownie has just one simple setting to make–then aim, press the button and you're making movies! Capturing your family good times in all their *action*... all their *color*... as only movies can.

And don't let the low price of the Brownie fool you, either. New simplified design, plus the Brownie's great popularity, helps us keep costs down. The Brownie is *all* camera, handsomely and ruggedly constructed for years of happy service.

Ask your dealer to show you the Brownie Movie Camera soon... And ask him about convenient terms, too. Most Kodak dealers offer them.

Disneyland's Grand Opening

17th July 1955

Guards at Sleeping Beauty's castle.

Original Mickey and Donald costumes, 17th July 1955.

Walt Disney at the opening ceremony. "To all who come to this happy place– welcome. Disneyland is your land."

Disneyland, Walt Disney's "folly" of fun, fantasy and futurism, opened its doors on 17th July 1955 for a special press preview. Chaos ensued after thousands of counterfeit tickets were sold. Uncontrollable crowds stormed the attractions, food and drink ran out, and underprepared facilities struggled to accommodate the hoards of excited attendees.

After several years of planning, the ambitious $17 million project was constructed in just one year on 16 acres in Anaheim, California. Despite its disastrous opening day, workers ensured all the park attractions were running smoothly within the month. And by the second month of operation, it was reported that 1 million people had visited. For most, it was and still is, "the happiest place on earth."

An estimated 70 million people tuned in to watch ABC TVs 90-minute live broadcast of the star-studded opening ceremonies, co-hosted by Ronald Reagan.

Advertisement

YOU'LL CALL IT "MILK MAGIC" — NEW INSTANT STARLAC

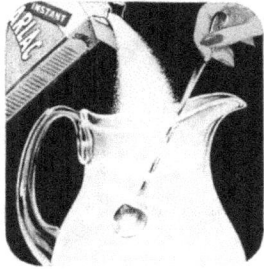

NEW Mixes instantly even in ice water!

NEW It tastes so good, you'll hardly believe you made it from a powder!

NEW true milk-sweet taste when compared with other brands

"The most exciting thing that's ever happened to milk," you'll say when you first try New Instant Starlac.

Think of it! You get all the proteins, B vitamins and calcium of the finest pasteurized milk for only about 8¢ a quart. What a saving! What a wonderful way to bring life-giving nourishment to your family at a low, low price!

This wonderful New Instant Starlac is put out by The Borden Company, the most famous name in milk, a company which has pioneered milk improvements for more than 100 years. Try New Instant Starlac. Get it at your grocer's today.

Use Borden's new-type nonfat milk for drinking, cooking and baking.

NEW packages... blue 5 qt. economy size... red 3 qt pre-measured.

NEW all new...mixes instantly, tastes better... you'll call it "Milk Magic"

In big blue economy 5-qt. pkg. for...

about 8¢ a quart

In red 3-qt. pre-measured envelope pkg. at a slightly higher price.

You'll call it "Milk Magic"—New Instant Starlac

• New. Mixes instantly even in ice water • New. It tastes so good, you'll hardly believe you made it from a powder! • New true milk-sweet taste when compared with other brands • New packages...blue 5qt. economy size...red 3qt. pre-measured. • New all new...mixes instantly, tastes better...you'll call it "Milk Magic"

"The most exciting thing that's ever happened to milk," you'll say when you first try New Instant Starlac. Think of it! You get all the proteins, B vitamins and calcium of the finest pasteurized milk for only about 8¢ a quart. What a saving! What a wonderful way to bring life-giving nourishment to your family at a low, low price!

This wonderful New Instant Starlac is put out by The Borden Company, the most famous name in milk, a company which has pioneered milk improvements for more than 100 years. Try New instant Starlac. Get it at your grocer's today.

Use Borden's new-type nonfat milk for drinking, cooking and baking.

In big blue economy 5-qt. pkg. for... about 8¢ a quart.
In red 3-qt. pre-measured envelope pkg. at a slightly higher price.

The Lord of the Rings Trilogy   29ᵗʰ Jul '54–20ᵗʰ Oct '55

The Lord of the Rings, a series of three fantasy novels written by English author J.R.R. Tolkien, was conceived as a sequel to his 1937 novel *The Hobbit*.

Originally written as one volume, the work was published as a trilogy in 1954-'55 in the UK, and 1955-'56 in the USA.

The Lord of the Rings immediate success was credited with the growing popularity of the fantasy genre from the '50s and '60s till the present day. Its influence on popular culture has been wide ranging, spawning many imitators in film, literature and video-gaming.

From 2001-2003 the books were released as a film series directed by Peter Jackson. Shot entirely in New Zealand, the films were a major critical and financial success. Each film garnered several Academy Awards, placing them among the greatest film trilogies ever made.

The Lord of the Rings has been translated in 38 different languages and sold over 150 million copies, remaining popular till this day. The books have been adapted for radio, theater, television and film. In 2003, the trilogy was awarded BBC's Best British novel of all time.

First Guinness Book of Records   27ᵗʰ August 1955

The first *Guinness Book of Records* arrived in bookstores across the UK on 27ᵗʰ August 1955. By Christmas it had become a crowd favorite and hot best seller. The second edition, released one year later, sold an astonishing 70,000 copies in the USA alone.

Sir Hugh Beaver, then the managing director of the Guinness Breweries, conceived the idea of a reference book to help settle nightly pub debates. The book would be filled with world records of human (and non-human) achievements.

Due to its immediate success, further books were released in the following years, settling into a pattern of one book per year.

Now known as *Guinness World Records*, the book itself holds the record of the best-selling copyrighted book of all time. It is published in 23 languages in over 100 countries, spawning multiple TV shows and franchised museums worldwide.

Hardcover, foreword and pages from the original *Guinness Book of Records*, 1955.

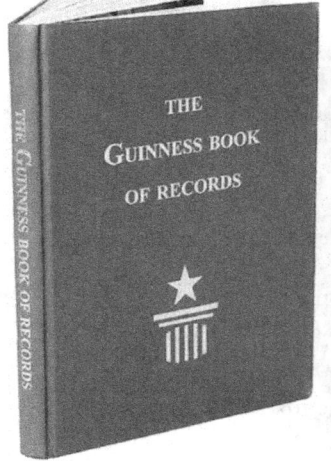
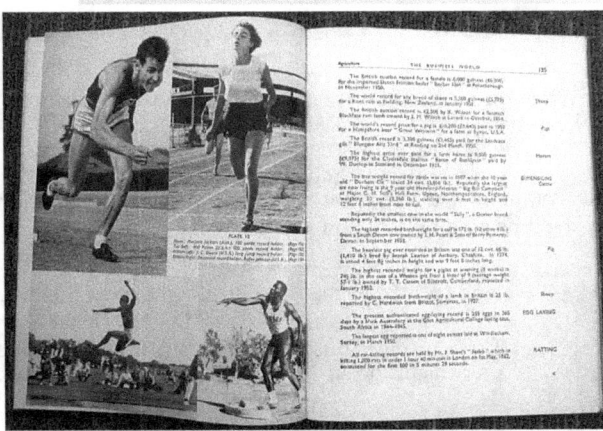

"Tell Daddy we miss him"

When one of the family is out of town, there's nothing like a regular telephone call to keep ties warm and close.

It's by far the fastest, easiest way to keep in touch...to share good news...to reach someone in a hurry. It means so much, it costs so little.

Why not call right now? It's easy–just tell the operator where you want to call: she'll be glad to help you.

Long distance rates are low. Here are some examples:

• Cleveland to Pittsburgh...45¢ • Birmingham to St. Louis...85¢ • Chicago to Buffalo...95¢ • Milwaukee to New York...$1.20 • San Francisco to Washington D.C...$2.00

These are the Station-to-Station rates for the first three minutes, after 6 o'clock every night and all day Sunday. They do not include the 10% federal excise tax.

Call by Number. It's Twice as Fast.

A Rock 'n' Roll Revolution

Rock 'n' roll exploded onto our soundwaves in the mid-'50s, and took the world by storm. The energy, the rhythm, the emotion—we had never heard anything quite like it before. Parents were alarmed and appalled in equal measure. It sprang from the ghettos of small town shop-front record studios while the big city record labels were napping.

Rock 'n' roll was the first music ever created specifically for teenagers. The first of the Baby Boomers had found their sound. It was neither black nor white. It gave expression to youth of any race and social status. It was a mash of rhythm & blues, country & western, gospel, hill-billy, blues, and jazz, with a heavy rock beat.

Chuck Berry, Fats Domino, Bill Haley and His Comets, Jerry Lee Lewis, and of course Elvis, became household names.

Jerry Lee Lewis.

Bill Haley and His Comets.

25th March 1955— *Blackboard Jungle* debuted with Bill Haley and His Comets *Rock Around the Clock* playing during the opening credits. The movie's soundtrack saw the largely teenage audience dancing in the aisles during screenings. This date is widely recognised as marking the birth of rock 'n' roll.

Sun Records in Memphis TN. was home to many rock 'n' roll greats, including Elvis Presley, Jerry Lee Lewis, Carl Perkins, Jonny Cash, Roy Orbison, Howlin' Wolf, and The Dixie Cups.

Billboard Top 30 Songs of 1955

	Artist	Song Title
1	Perez Prado	Cherry Pink And Apple Blossom White
2	Bill Haley & His Comets	Rock Around the Clock
3	Mitch Miller	The Yellow Rose of Texas
4	Roger Williams	Autumn Leaves
5	Les Baxter	Unchained Melody
6	Bill Hayes	The Ballad of Davy Crockett
7	The Four Aces	Love Is a Many-Splendored Thing
8	The McGuire Sisters	Sincerely
9	Pat Boone	Ain't That a Shame
10	Georgia Gibbs	The Wallflower (Dance with Me, Henry)

Perez Prado.

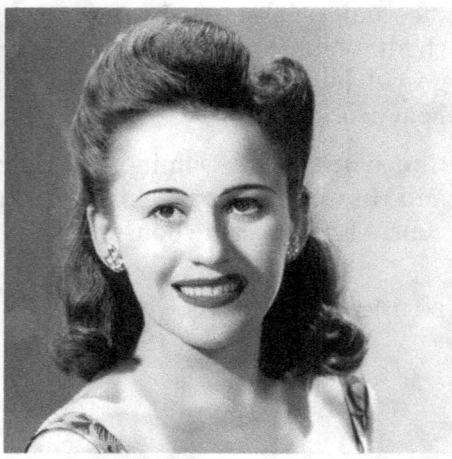

Georgia Gibbs.

Pat Boone.

Roger Williams.

	Artist	Song Title
11	Johnny Maddox	The Crazy Otto Medley
12	Billy Vaughn	Melody of Love
13	Tennessee Ernie Ford	Sixteen Tons
14	Frank Sinatra	Learnin' the Blues
15	The Fontane Sisters	Hearts of Stone
16	Georgia Gibbs	Tweedle Dee
17	The Four Lads	Moments to Remember
18	The Chordettes	Mr. Sandman
19	Joan Weber	Let Me Go, Lover!
20	Nat King Cole	A Blossom Fell

Frank Sinatra, 1957.

Nat King Cole, 1958.

	Artist	Song Title
21	Al Hibbler	Unchained Melody
22	Fess Parker	The Ballad of Davy Crockett
23	Art Mooney	Honey-Babe
24	Tennessee Ernie Ford	The Ballad of Davy Crockett
25	Perry Como	Ko Ko Mo (I Love You So)
26	Gisele MacKenzie	Hard to Get
27	Ames Brothers	The Naughty Lady of Shady Lane
28	Jaye P. Morgan	That's All I Want from You
29	The Platters	Only You (And You Alone)
30	Somethin' Smith & the Redheads	It's a Sin to Tell a Lie

*From the *Billboard* top 30 singles of 1955.

Advertisement

Fashion's new pet...our Poodle Print only 5.98

Fashion's pet... and yours! Our adorable new border "poodle print" is the cutest thing around town! "Stop-look" styling... with curved lines, tiny middle and big tiered skirt.
You'll have it for movie dates... informal parties. It's sure to rate with the crowd... send admiring glances your way. Big fashion... the little price? Only $5.98!

Fashion Trends of the 1950s

With the misery and bleakness of the war years behind us, it was now time to show off. Consumerism was a way of life and we were all too willing to spend money on luxuries, non-essentials, and fashion.

How we looked and how we dressed became important everyday considerations for women and men. We spent money like never before, guided by our favorite fashion icons, and helped along by a maturing advertising industry which flooded us with fashion advice through newspapers, magazines, billboards, radio and television.

Dress by Anne Fogarty, Summer 1955.

Clothing manufacturers had perfected mass production techniques while providing military uniforms during the war years. They now shifted their focus to well made, stylish, ready-to-wear clothes.

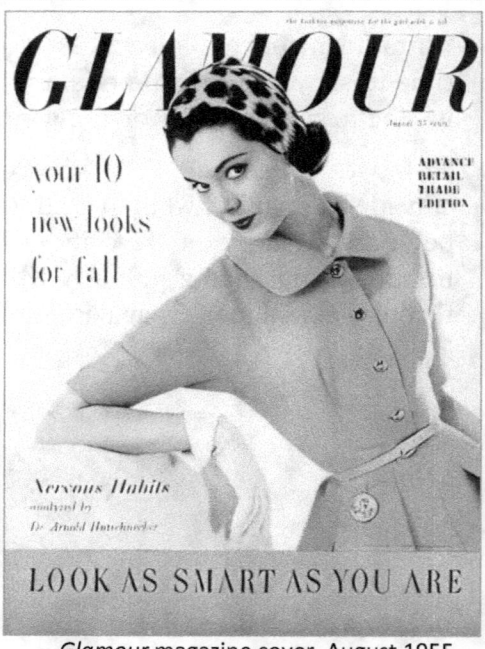

Glamour magazine cover, August 1955.

Harper's Bazaar magazine cover, July 1955.

Vogue magazine cover, February 1955.

Fashion was no longer a luxury reserved for the wealthy. Now the growing middle class could also afford to be fashionable. Magazines and mail-order catalogs kept us informed of the latest trends in fashion, make-up, and accessories.

Dresses from the *Bellas Hess Spriing-Summer 1955* mail order catalog in the "New Look" style that was popular in the 1950s.

Advertisement

It's simply <u>wicked</u> what it does for you

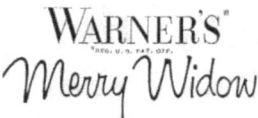
WARNER'S
Merry Widow

Care to be daring, darling? To look outright naughty, yet feel downright nice? Then why not give in to that inner whisper, and agree to star in this exciting new vehicle.

You'll get all the best lines... all the admiring looks—in your most demanding clothes. Your entrances? Positively breathtaking. Because Warner's knows every beautiful scene-stealing way to keep you in the center of the stage.

Once you taste the spotlights and applause, you'll never go anywhere *important* without your Merry Widow. Here just two of the famous supporting cast. Try the feeling today! From $3.50 at the nicest stores here and in Canada.

#1311. (*Right*) The fabulous original... for a hand-span waist, a grand-stand look. Cuffs turn down or up. Black or white embroidered nylon and elastic marquisette, $12.50.

#1317. (*Left*) The waist a little easier, the lines a little longer; the bust high, round, and youthful for the newest dresses. Black or white embroidered nylon marquisette. $15.00.

Christian Dior's "New Look" from 1947.

The New Look in *Vanity Fair*, May 1953.

As with before the war, all eyes looked to Paris for new trends in haute couture. In 1947 Christian Dior didn't disappoint, unveiling his ultra-feminine, glamorous, extravagant, "New Look".

Gone were the boxy tailored jackets with padded shoulders and slim, short skirts. Paris had brought back femininity, with clinched waists, fuller busts and hips, and longer, wider skirts.

By 1954, dresses reached voluminous proportions with pleats and folds flaunting an abundance of fabric. The New Look set the standard for the entire decade of the 1950s.

how clever!

EVEN THE WIRE IS CURVED TO STAY UP!

CELEBRITY does more than give you deep-plunging separation... CELEBRITY curves the wiring of this strapless bra to make the uplift STAY UP! No tugging, no pulling, no displacement! Get marvelous up-curve flattery in heavenly comfort. White rayon satin, or white cotton.

A Cup, sizes 32 to 36
B Cup, sizes 32 to 38
$1.50

Celebrity "CONTOUR-CURVE STITCHING"
from the bottom up

To achieve this impossible hourglass figure, corsets and girdles were sold in record numbers. Metal underwire bras made a comeback, and a new form of bra known as the "cathedral bra" or "bullet bra" became popular.

Despite criticisms against the extravagance of the New Look, and arguments that heavy corsets and paddings undermined the freedoms women had won during the war years, the New Look was embraced on both sides of the Atlantic. Before long, inexpensive, ready-to-wear versions of Dior's New Look had found their way into our department store catalogs.

Patterns from *Haslam Dresscutting Book No. 31,* Summer 1954.

Advertisement

You can get a smoother tan... faster with Skol's exclusive formula

Tan gloriously

your first day in the sun
...with **SKOL'S** sun-control screen

- you don't burn
- you don't peel
- no messy oil

Skol's sun-control screen actually *regulates* the sun's effect on your skin. It shuts out the harmful burning rays. Lets in the beneficial tanning rays. Speeds up the whole tanning process—more *safely*.

You tan comfortably

Not a trace of oil or grease to get on your suit or towel or beach bag. Skol goes on cleanly, neatly. Doesn't pick up sand. And Skol is kind to your skin. Skol won't dry out natural moisture. Won't leave your skin feeling drawn and "tight."

More people tan with Skol

Originally formulated for Alpine guides to prevent dreaded "snow-burn," Skol has become the leading sun product throughout the world. Swimmers, golfers, skiers, all people who play and work in the sun choose Skol above all others.

Use the new Skol this summer. You'll tan *faster* ... in a day or a weekend. More *beautifully* ... and safely. Get your bottle of Skol today. Also available in plastic bottles.

Tan gloriously–your first day in the sun...with SKOL's sun-control screen
• you don't burn • you don't peel • no messy oil

Skol's sun-control screen actually *regulates* the sun's effect on your skin. It shuts out the harmful burning rays. Lets in the beneficial tanning rays. Speeds up the whole tanning process–more *safely*.
You tan comfortable.
Not a trace of oil or grease to get on your suit or towel or beach bag. Skol goes on cleanly, neatly. Doesn't pick up sand. And Skol is kind to your skin. Skol won't dry out natural moisture. Won't leave your skin feeling drawn and "tight."
More people tan with Skol.
Originally formulated for Alpine guides to prevent dreaded "snow-burn," Skol has become the leading sun product throughout the world. Swimmers, golfers, skiers, all people who play and work in the sun choose Skol above all others.
Use the new Skol this summer. You'll tan *faster*... in a day or a weekend. More *beautifully*... and safely. Get your bottle of Skol today. Also available in plastic bottles.

Dior also created a slimmed down alternative look, widely copied by other designers in ready-to-wear outfits and pattern books. This figure-hugging, groomed and tailored look continued to place emphasis on the hourglass figure, and was suitable for day or evening dress, or as an elegant straight skirt and short jacket.

Known as the "sheath dress" or "wiggle dress", this sexier figure-hugging silhouette was preferred by movie stars such as Marilyn Monroe.

Women embraced the femininity of 1950s fashion from head to toe. Hats, scarves, belts, gloves, shoes, stockings, handbags and jewelry were all given due consideration.

Out on the street, no outfit would be complete without a full complement of matching accessories.

Not much changed in the world of men's fashion during the 1950s. Business attire shifted just a little. Suits were slimmer, and ties were narrower. Skinny belts were worn over pleated pants. Hats, though still worn, were on the way out.

Frank Sinatra.

Marlon Brando.

James Dean.

For the younger generation however, the fashion icons of the day set the trends. James Dean and Marlon Brando made the white T-shirt and blue jeans the must-have items in casual attire. Worn alone, or under an unbuttoned shirt or jacket, the look made working class style a middle-class fashion statement.

Advertisement

Surprise! It's liltingly light, yet lusciously bright!
We fervently feel that pink is for girls... and a million men agree with us! "Love That Pink!"... not a shy pink... a showoff pink! Not a whisper pink, a whistle pink! It's light, yet it's bright (what a beautiful paradox!) No matter what your coloring, this is your color! Whether you're petal-pale or brown as bronze, wear "Love That Pink" tonight... you'll hear the excitement crackling, clear across the room!

Advertisement

They fit you better than your own skin!
Bur-Mil Cameo Shape-2-U sheer nylon stretch stockings
They look better and feel more comfortable than any stockings you've ever worn
New, Bur-Mil Cameo Shape-2-U stockings stretch from top-to-toe to fit you perfectly...to hug every part of your leg. No more wrinkles, no crooked seams! Long-wearing Shape-2-U are the most comfortable stockings you've ever worn. And they're sheer–beautifully, breathlessly sheer.
You'll love the flattering "Skin Tone" colors, the glamour of misty-dull "Face Powder Finish," too. Bur-Mil Cameo Shape-2-U in three personally proportioned sizes–one perfect for you. At the nicest stores. $1.95.

A Vaccine for Polio

During the first half of the 20th Century the dreaded poliomyelitis virus (polio) caused frequent epidemics throughout the industrialized world. The virus appeared during the summer months, attacking mostly the young, causing muscle weakness, paralysis and death.

Jonas Salk's polio vaccine, widely tested in field trials during the preceding year, was declared safe for use on 12th April 1955. A nationwide inoculation program began in the USA, reducing the number of polio cases by 90% within just two years.

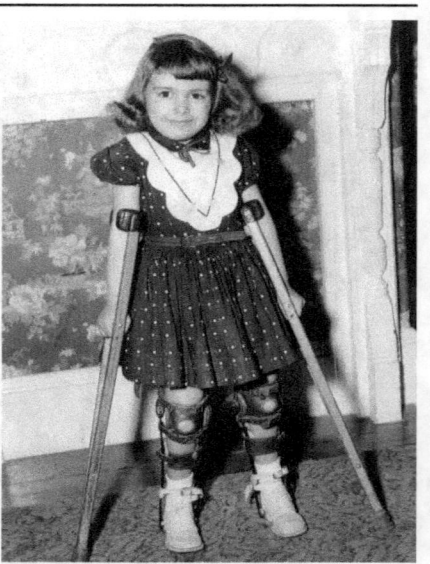

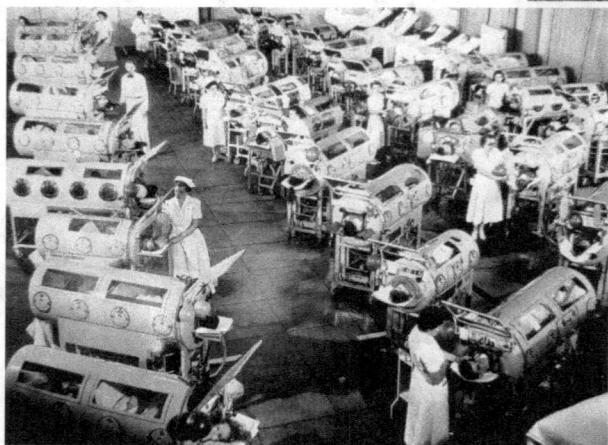

At its peak in the '40s and '50s, polio affected many thousands of people each year. Use of the "iron lung" a pressure chamber to aid breathing, saved the lives of those with infected lungs. Patients were encased within for months, years, or even for life.

Rows of polio patients in their iron lungs at the Rancho Los Amigos hospital in Downey, Calif. 1953.

To save on floor space within polio wards, children were placed in iron lung "pods"— multi-person negative-pressure ventilators.

Worldwide polio eradication is still an ongoing struggle, as some developing countries continue to see yearly outbreaks of the virus. Civil wars, ignorance, and government distrust prevent large scale vaccination programs from succeeding.

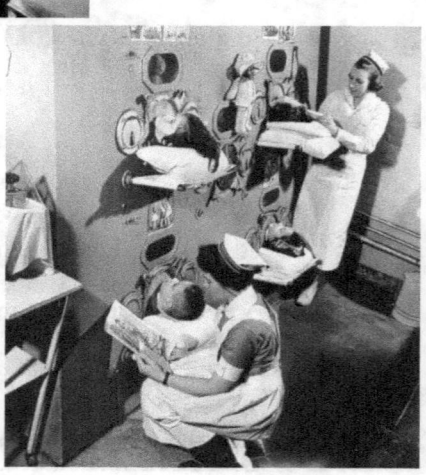

Science and Medicine

15th Feb– Howard Tracy Hall, working for the General Electric Company, announced the successful creation of synthetic diamonds in the scientific journal *Nature*, with a reproducible, verifiable and well-documented process.

15th Mar– The United States Air Force unveiled its first supersonic air-to-surface self-guided missile–the GAM-63 RASCAL.

The RASCAL required an air-launch above 40,000 feet (12,000 m). A computer within tracked the aircraft position against a pre-programmed target, automatically releasing the missile at the launch point. The missile would continue climbing for a certain distance, before diving on its target.

7th Aug– Sony began selling the TR-55 transistor radio– the first commercial transistor radio to utilize all miniature components.

11th Oct– *Oklahoma!* debuted using the new 70-mm wide film system known as the Todd-AO. Developed by producer Mike Todd, the 70mm was much cheaper to run than its wide film predecessor Cinerama.

1955– The first cesium based atomic clock was built at the National Physical Laboratory, UK. by Louis Essen and Jack Parry. The clock became commercially available, for use as a calibration source, the following year. It cost $20,000.

Other News from 1955

1955– Coca-Cola expanded its size offerings introducing bottles in 10-, 12-, 16-, and 26-ounce sizes. Before this, only the standard 6.5-ounce bottle had been available. Coke also began manufacturing its first canned drinks for sale to overseas armed services. A protective polymer lining added to the inside of the can prevented the steel from acid erosion.

2nd Jan– Panamanian president José Antonio Remón was assassinated by three assailants armed with sub-machine guns. His successor, José Ramón Guizado, was later arrested for orchestrating the assassination. Guizado would spend thirty-three months in jail before being acquitted.

17th Jan– USS Nautilus (SSN-571) became the world's first nuclear powered submarine. Able to remain submerged longer than traditional diesel-electric submarines, she could travel to depths previously unattainable, and cruise at faster speed.

24th Feb– Severe weather in Britain plunged temperatures below freezing leaving more than 70 roads blocked with snow and Country rail services canceled. Snowdrifts as high as 30ft (9m) were recorded.

1st Mar– Pakistan and India drew in the 5th cricket Test at the National Stadium in Karachi; 5 Test series, score 0-0.

5th Apr– British Prime Minister Winston Churchill resigned due to ill-health at the age of 80. Churchill had served as Prime Minister from 1940-1945, and again from 1951-1955.

11th Apr– An assassination attempt on Premier Zhou Enlai left sixteen dead when a bomb exploded on the chartered plane supposed to be carrying the Chinese leader. He was not on board.

6th Jun– British Parliament introduced the Harmful Publications Act, aimed at protecting children from violent, repulsive or horror comics.

5th May– 10 years after the end of WWII, West Germany was granted full sovereignty by its three occupying Allied powers. Military occupation ended, and West Germany joined NATO on 9th May 1955.

11th Jun– Eighty-three spectators were killed and 180 more injured after two race cars collided in the 24 Hours of Le Mans, France. Flying and burning debris were hurled into the stands at high speed. The race remains known as auto-racing's deadliest day.

15th Sep– Vladimir Nabokov's controversial novel Lolita was published by Olympia Press, Paris. The book was soon banned in France and the UK. It sold 100,000 copies in its first three weeks of release in the USA in 1958.

The novel has since been adapted for stage, film, ballet, opera and Broadway.

22nd Sep– Commercial television started in the UK when the Independent Television Authority's (ITV) began broadcasting in London, ending the BBC monopoly.

Advertisement

How to avoid dry, unruly "jungle hair"

New greaseless way to keep your hair neat all day

New Vitalis with V-7 prevents dryness, makes hair easy to manage

If you dislike over-oily hair tonics, here's good news. New Vitalis keeps hair in place with V-7, the *greaseless* grooming discovery.

You can use Vitalis as often as you like — even every day — yet never have an over-slick, plastered-down look.

What's more, it gives you wonderful protection from dry hair and scalp. And tests show it kills on contact germs many doctors associate with infectious dandruff — as no mere cream or oil dressing can.

Try new Vitalis with V-7. You'll *like* it.

New VITALIS® Hair Tonic with V-7®

"TISSUE TEST" proves greaseless Vitalis outdates messy oils

In an independent testing laboratory, Vitalis and leading cream and oil tonics were applied in the normal way. Hair was combed and then wiped with cleansing tissue. Unretouched photographs above show the difference in results!

ANOTHER FINE PRODUCT OF BRISTOL-MYERS

How to avoid dry, unruly, "jungle hair".
New greaseless way to keep your hair neat all day.

New Vitalis with V-7 prevents dryness, makes hair easy to mange.

If you dislike over-oily hair tonics, here's good news. New Vitalis keeps hair in place with V-7, the *greaseless* grooming discovery.

You can use Vitalis as often as you like—even every day—yet never have an over-slick, plastered-down look. What's more, it gives you wonderful protection from dry hair and scalp. And tests show it kills on contact germs many doctors associate with infectious dandruff—as no mere cream or oil dressing can.

Try new Vitalis with V-7. You'll *like* it.

"Tissue Test" proves greaseless Vitalis outdates messy oils.

In an independent testing laboratory, Vitalis and leading cream and oil tonics were applied in the normal way. Hair was combed and then wiped with cleansing tissue. Unretouched photographs above show the difference in results!

Advertisement

"Is this something special?"   "It certainly is... that's Ballantine Ale"

The sociable beverage that's more and more in evidence at friendly gatherings is Ballantine... the *different* ale.

In Ballantine, the time-honored flavor of ale... and the lightness and liveliness Americans prefer in their brewed beverages... are so happily married that it has won a very special place in the affections of millions.

The sooner you try it, the longer you'll have to enjoy it. Get acquainted with this great ale today; it gives you so much more in flavor... and satisfaction... *it's America's favorite by four to one.*

Famous People Born in 1955

6th Jan– Rowan Atkinson, English comedian & actor.

18th Jan– Kevin Costner, American actor, producer & director.

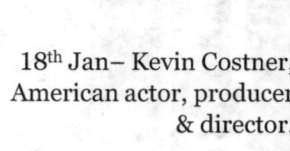

28th Jan– Nicolas Sarkozy, 23rd President of France.

8th Feb– John Grisham, American writer, attorney & politician.

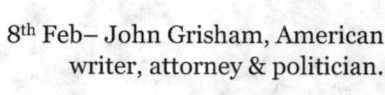

10th Feb– Greg Norman, Australian golfer.

21st Feb– Kelsey Grammer, American actor & comedian.

24th Feb– Alain Prost, French Formula One racing driver.

24th Feb– Steve Jobs, American computer entrepreneur & co-founder of Apple.

5th Mar– Penn Jillette, American author and magician (Penn & Teller).

19th Mar– Bruce Willis, American actor.

23rd Mar– Moses Malone, Basketball Hall of Fame center.

31st Mar– Angus Young, Scottish Australian, rock guitarist (ACDC).

15th Apr– Dodi Fayed, Egyptian businessman.

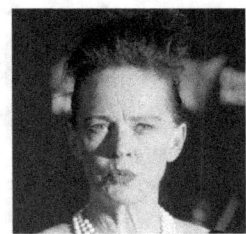

23rd Apr– Judy Davis, Australian actress.

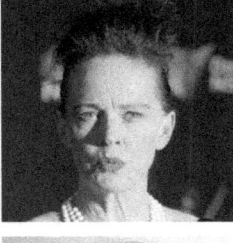

2nd May– Donatella Versace, Italian fashion designer.

3rd May– David Hookes, Australian cricketer.

16th May– Jack Morris, Baseball Hall of Fame pitcher.

18th May– Chow Yun-Fat, Hong Kong actor.

7th Jun– William Forsythe, American actor.

8th Jun– Tim Berners-Lee, English inventor of the World Wide Web.

22nd Jul– Willem Dafoe, American actor.

25th Jul– Iman Abdulmajid, Somalian fashion model.

4th Aug– Billy Bob Thornton, American actor, director & screenwriter.

13th Aug– Betsy King, American golfer.

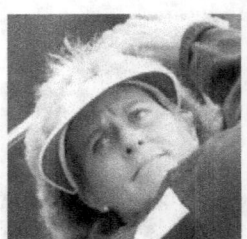

15th Sep– Renzo Rosso, Italian clothing designer.

28th Oct– Bill Gates, American businessman.

6th Nov– Maria Shriver, American newscaster.

13th Nov– Whoopi Goldberg, American actress & comedian.

24th Nov– Ian Botham, England cricket captain, all-rounder.

27th Nov– Bill Nye, the Science Guy, TV Host.

29th Nov– Howie Mandel, comedian.

30th Nov– Billy Idol, [William Broad], rocker.

30th Nov– Deborah-lee Furness, Australian Actress.

Advertisement

WHAT'S NEW?

A new fine-strand spaghetti with beefy little meatballs—by Franco-American

My goodness, hadn't you heard? Here's a brand-new Franco-American dish that's different from anything you've ever tasted. Different, and (forgive us for bragging) terrific! It's our special new Spaghetti with Meatballs.

This is a *fine-strand* spaghetti—the kind you like so much—in a tantalizing new tomato sauce. But the best news is about those tender, beefy little meatballs you see in our picture. They're *already in the Spaghetti.* Four of them—count 'em, four—in every single can! This is a *meal,* Mothers. Mighty nutritious eating, too. Don't forget that every helping supplies *proteins* and *energy* which growing children and grownups need every day.

Like all your old Franco-American favorites, this newest treat is a cinch to fix. You simply heat it for about 3 minutes, serve, and get ready to say, "Thank you," for all the compliments you'll get.

Economical? Very agreeably so. It costs less than 15¢ a serving.

1955 in Numbers

Census Statistics [1]

- Population of the world   2.77 billion
- Population in the United States   171.69 million
- Population in the United Kingdom   51.06 million
- Population in Canada   15.67 million
- Population in Australia   9.17 million
- Average age for marriage of women   20.2 years old
- Average age for marriage of men   22.6 years old
- Average family income USA $4,400 per year
- Minimum wage USA $0.75 per hour

Costs of Goods [2]

- Average home — $18,346
- Average new car — $1,900
- Studebaker Commander Coupe — $2,095
- A gallon of gasoline — $0.29
- A loaf of bread — $0.18
- A gallon of milk — $0.92
- Oreo cookies — $0.39 per pkg
- Sirloin chops — $0.69 per pound
- Starkist tuna — $0.25 per 6.5 oz can
- Potatoes — $0.53 for 10 pounds
- Large eggs — $0.61 per dozen
- Nylons — $1.00 a pair
- Ivory soap — $0.29 for 2 bars

---

[1] Figures from worldometers.info/world-population, US National Center for Health Statistics, *Divorce and Divorce Rates* US (cdc.gov/nchs/data/series/sr_21/sr21_029.pdf) and US Census Bureau, *Historical Marital Status Tables* (census.gov/data/tables/time-series/demo/families/ marital.html).
[2] Figures from thepeoplehistory.com, mclib.info/reference/local-history and dqydj.com/historical-home-prices/.

Great day in the morning! Flavor in a filter cigarette!
Winston tastes good–like a cigarette should!
Winston brings flavor back to filter smoking!

No wonder Winston has changed America's mind about filter cigarettes! Winston tastes good–like a cigarette should! It's got a real flavor–the full, rich flavor real smokers want. You're sure to enjoy Winston's finer flavor!

Winston also introduced a finer filter that works so effectively, yet doesn't "thin" the taste. The fine tobacco flavor comes clean thru to you because Winstons are easy-drawing. You'll really appreciate Winston's finer filter!

Smoke Winston *the easy-drawing filter cigarette!*

Advertisement

More people travel by Greyhound than by any other transportation system
...because millions find Greyhound Today's Best Buy in Travel!

About 150 million passengers took intercity trips by Greyhound Bus last year–millions more than by any other transportation system–land, sea or air!

"Intercity" travel means "between cities"–and doesn't include local trips. Counting commuters, Greyhound carries nearly 200 million passengers yearly!

This may be news to many–but to people who travel regularly by Greyhound, it isn't surprising. For no other form of transportation can give you so much real down-to-earth value for your money...so many scenic miles for a dollar–such frequent schedules–so much relaxed comfort.

What's more, Greyhound is the only travel system that can take you on one ticket, with one high standard of service, to every great American city, every one of the 48 states, and into Canada and Mexico!

Can you wonder that Greyhound is America's most popular transportation?

There's something about a Greyhound that makes it the Friendly way to travel!

These words first appeared in print in the year 1955.

- Microwave oven
- gangbusters
- Artificial Intelligence
- fabric softener
- counterintuitive
- Big Bang Theory
- certified mail
- Fallout Shelter
- DIY
- Information Science
- mind-boggling
- AEROSPACE
- Intensive Care Unit
- home computer
- SPECIAL FORCES
- STRESS TEST
- skydiving

* From merriam-webster.com/time-traveler/1955.

A heartfelt plea from the author:

I sincerely hope you enjoyed reading this book and that it brought back many fond memories from the past.

Success as an author has become increasingly difficult with the proliferation of **AI generated** copycat books by unscrupulous sellers. They are clever enough to escape copyright action and use dark web tactics to secure paid-for **fake reviews**, something I would never do.

Hence I would like to ask you—I plead with you—the reader, to leave a star rating or review on Amazon. This helps make my book discoverable for new readers, and helps me to compete fairly against the devious copycats.

If this book was a gift to you, you can leave stars or a review on your own Amazon account, or you can ask the gift-giver or a family member to do this on your behalf.

I have enjoyed researching and writing this book for you and would greatly appreciate your feedback.

Best regards,
Bernard Bradforsand-Tyler.

Please leave a
book review/rating at:

https://bit.ly/1955-reviews

Or scan the QR code:

Flashback books make the perfect gift- see the full range at

https://bit.ly/FlashbackSeries

Image Attributions

Photographs and images used in this book are reproduced courtesy of the following:

Page 6 – Source: americanhistory.si.edu/blog/2011/10/food-culture.html. Pre-1978 (PD image).
Page 8 – From *Life* Mag, 7th Nov 1955. Source: books.google.com/books?id=xFQEAAAAMBAJ&printsec (PD image).*
Page 9 – Image cropped from Mutual of New York advertisement printed in *Life* magazine 7th Mar 1955. Source: books.google.com/books?id=JFQEAAAAMBAJ&printsec. (PD image).*
Page 10 – Source: ushistoryscene.com/article/levittown/. Pre-1978, no copyright mark (PD image).
Page 11 – Advertisement source: ebay.com. Pre-1978, no copyright mark (PD image).*
Page 12 – From *Life* mag, 7th Mar 1955. Source: books.google.com/books?id=JFQEAAAAMBAJ&printsec. (PD image).*
Page 13 – Leadenhall Street from Bishopsgate, 1955. Creative Commons license. Photo by Ben Brooksbank.
Page 14 – From *Life* Mag, 4th July 1955. Source: books.google.com/books?id=r1YEAAAAMBAJ&printsec. (PD image).*
Page 15 – Private image, unknown creator. Pre-1978, no copyright mark (PD image).
Page 16 – From *Life* Mag, 4th July 1955. Source: books.google.com/books?id=r1YEAAAAMBAJ&printsec. (PD image).*
Page 17 – General Motors carpark, source: books.google.com./books?id=r1YEAAAAMBAJ&printsec. (PD image).
Page 18 – Imperial by Chrysler, *Life* magazine, 25th July 1955. Source: books.google.com/books?id=wIYEAAAAMBAJ&printsec. – Studebaker advertisement, *Life* magazine, 14th Mar 1955. Source: books.google.com/books?id= A1QEAAAAMBAJ &printsec. – Mercury by Ford advertisement, *Life* magazine, 21st Feb 1955. Source: books.google.com/books?id= LFQEAAAAMBAJ&printsec. All images this page (PD images).*
Page 19 – Source: flickr.com/photos/aussiefordadverts/5205760405/. Attrib-NoDerivatives 4.0 Int (CC BY-ND 4.0).
Page 20 – From *Life* mag, 28th Feb 1955. Source: books.google.com/books?id=QIQEAAAAMBAJ&printsec. (PD image).*
Page 21 – MG MGA, 1955-'56. Source: flickr.com/photos/andreboeni/40154877544/. – SAAB 93, 1955. Source: flickr.com/ photos/andreboeni/33663136616/. – Pegaso Z-103, 1955. Source: flickr.com/photos/andreboeni/ 28097457979/. All photos Attribution 4.0 International (CC BY 4.0). – Chevrolet Assembly line, 1955. This image is the property of General Motors, printed here under fair use terms for information only, as it is significant to the article created. It is rendered in low resolution to avoid piracy. It is believed that this will not in any way limit the ability of the copyright owners to market or sell the product.
Page 22 – From *Life* mag, 7th Mar 1965. Source: books.google.com/books?id=JFQEAAAAMBAJ&printsec. (PD image).*
Page 23 – '50s family, source: flickr.com/photos/brizzlebornandbred/23023833354. Attribution 4.0 (Creative Commons (CC) BY 4.0). – Publicity photo from *Warner Brothers Presents*, 1955 by Warner Brothers.** Source: imdb.com/title/tt0047786/ mediaviewer/rm3026790144.
Page 24 – Screen still from *The $64,000 Question*, 1955 by CBS Television.** – Publicity photo for *General Electric Theatre*, 1955 by CBS TV. Source: en.wikipedia.org/wiki/General_Electric_Theater. Pre-1978, no mark (PD image).
Page 25 – Screen still from *The Millionaire*, 8th July 1957, by CBS Television.** Source: commons.wikimedia.org/wiki/ File: Angie_Dickenson_ James_Craig_The_Millionaire_1957.JPG. – The original Mouseketeers from first week of *The Mickey Mouse Club*, 3rd Oct 1955.** – Screen still from *Gunsmoke* circa 1955, by CBS Television.** Source: imdb.com/ title/tt0047736/mediaviewer/rm929144065. – Screen still from *The Adventures of Robin Hood* by Sapphire Films.**
Page 26 – From *Life* Mag, 4th July 1955. Source: books.google.com/books?id=r1YEAAAAMBAJ&printsec. (PD image).*
Page 27 – Source: dailymail.co.uk/femail/article-5249797/Adverts-1940s-50s-60s-world-changed. Pre-'78 (PD image).
Page 28 – Lawyers Hayes, Marshall and Nabrit at the Supreme Court, 17th May 1954. Source: commons.wikimedia. org/wiki/Category:Brown_v._Board_of_Education (PD image). – Newspaper headlines following the Till murder.
Page 29 – Rosa Parks with Dr. King printed in *Ebony* Magazine, 1955. Source: en.wikipedia.org/wiki/Rosa_Parks from United States Information Agency (Bureau of Public Affairs). Pre-1978, no copyright mark (PD image).
– Parks riding a bus, 21st Dec 1965, source: loc.gov/pictures/item/94505572/ from the Library of Congress, (PD image). – Parks fingerprinted by Lieutenant D.H. Lackey, 22nd Feb 1956 (PD image). – Bus 2857, source: en.wikipedia.org/wiki/Rosa_Parks. CC BY-SA 3.0. – Parks statue in the National Civil Rights Museum, Memphis, TN. Source: commons.wikimedia.org/wiki/File:Rosa_parks_ human_rights_museum_memphis_2.jpg. CC Attribution-Share Alike 4.0 International. – Parks statue at US Capitol by Eugene Daub, 2013. Source: aoc.gov/explore-capitol-campus/art/rosa-parks. (PD image).
Page 30 – Missile launch, this image is the work of the U.S. federal government. Pre-1978, no mark (PD image).
Page 31 – CIDG unit training. Source: pbs.org/kenburns/the-vietnam-war/episodes/and en.wikipedia.org/wiki/Civilian _ Irregular_ Defense_Group_program. This image is a work of the U.S. federal government. Pre-1978 (PD image).
Page 32 – From *Life* Mag, 7th Feb 1955. Source: books.google.com/books?id=6VMEAAAAMBAJ&printsec. (PD image).*
Page 33 – Poster images from BOAC and BEA, 1955.**
Page 34 – MacDonalds, creators unknown. Pre-1978, no copyright mark (PD image).
Page 35 – *The Daily Princetonian* extra edition released 18th Apr 1955. Pre-1978, no copyright mark (PD image).
– Einstein in 1947 from the United States Library of Congress Prints and Photographs division digital ID cph.3b46036, source: commons.wikimedia.org/wiki/File:Albert_Einstein_Head.jpg. (PD image).
Page 36 – Juan Perón, source: en.wikipedia.org/wiki/Juan_Perón#/media/File:Juan_Perón_1946.jpg. (PD image).
– Eva Perón, source: commons.wikimedia.org/wiki/File:Evita_con_traje_formal.jpg. (PD image).
Page 37 – From *Life* mag, 7th Mar 1955. Source: books.google.com/books?id=JFQEAAAAMBAJ&printsec. (PD image).*

Page 38 – Screen still from *Vertigo* by Paramount Pictures, 1958.** Source: commons.wikimedia.org/wiki/Fi e:Kim_ Novak_ James_Stewart_Vertigo_Still.jpg. – Newman studio publicity still, source: en.wikipedia.org/wiki/Paul_ Newman#/media/File:Paul_Newman_1954.JPG. Pre-1978, no copyright mark (PD image). – Eastwood, creator unknown, circa 1955. Source: reddit.com/r/OldSchoolCool/comments/fnkucq/a_dashing_young_clint_eastwood_ 1955/ by u/langator. (PD image).
Page 39 – Marilyn Monroe publicity photo for *The Seven Year Itch*, 1955 by Twentieth Century-Fox. Source: en.wikipedia.org/wiki/The_Seven_Year_Itch#/media/File:Marilyn_Monroe_photo_pose_Seven_Year_Itch.jpg. (PD image). – *Guys and Dolls* poster, 1955, by MGM.** Source: famousfix.com/topic/guys-and-dolls. – *Lady and the Tramp* movie poster, 1955, by Disney.** Source: posteritati.com/poster/47783/lady-and-the-tramp-1955-us-herald.
Page 40 – James Dean, source: needpix.com/photo/222883. Pre-1978, no copyright mark (PD image). – Dean in his Spyder, and news footage of the crash site. Source: wikimapia.org/2254780/James-Dean-s-fatal-car-accident-actual-site. Images are included here for information only under U.S. fair use laws due to: 1- No free alternative ex sts of the event; 2- images are low resolution copies; 3- these do not limit the copyright owner's rights to sell the products in any way; 4- Copies are too small to be used to make illegal copies for another book; 5- The images are significant to the article created.
Page 41 – James Dean in *East of Eden* and *Rebel Without a Cause*, 1955, by Warner Bros.** Source: en.wikipedia.org/wiki/James_Dean. – James Dean In *Giant*, 1956, by Warner Bros.** Source: flickr.com/photos/elizafairy/3683651704. Attribution 4.0 International (CC BY 4.0).
Page 42 – Lockheed Super Constellation print advertisement, source: eBay (PD image).*
Page 43 – Ad Source: vintageadbrowser.com/photography-ads-1950s/9. Pre-1978, no copyright renewal (PD image).
Page 44 – *Cat on a Hot Tin Roof* Theatre poster, 1955.** Source: wnyc.org/story/cat-on-a-hot-tin-roof/. – Stage and film montage, source: broadway.com/buzz/166691/cats-meow-how-tennessee-williams-cat-on-a-hot-tin-roof-keeps-prowling-back-to-broadway/. Pre-1978, no copyright mark (PD image). – Movie poster, 1958, by MGM.** Source: en.wikipedia.org/wiki/Cat_ on_a_Hot_Tin_Roof_(1958_film).
Page 45 – Ad Source: jana-treeclimber.blogspot.com/2012/09/. Pre-1978, no copyright renewal (PD image).
Page 46 – Family at Disneyland, Anaheim, California, 1956. Source: flickr.com/photos/iisg/4586688368/. Attribution-ShareAlike 4.0 International (CC BY-SA 4.0). – Original Mickey and Donald, 17th July 1955. Source: flickr.com/photos/iisg/ 4586688368. Attribution-ShareAlike 4.0 International (CC BY-SA 4.0). – Walt Disney, 17th July 1955. Source: thisdayin disneyhistory.com/DisneylandGrandOpening.html. Creator unknown, no copyright mark (PD image). – Ronald Reagan, screen still from *Dateline: Disneyland* on ABC.** Source: yesterland.com/dl1955.html.
Page 47 – From *Life* Mag 14th Feb 1955. Source: books.google.com/books?id=N1QEAAAAMBAJ&printsec (PD image).*
Page 48 – *Lord of the Rings* books,** source: abebooks.com/rare-books/most-expensive-sales/year-2015.shtml?cm_sp. – *Lord of the Rings* movie posters, 2001-2003, by New Line Cinema.**
Page 49 – Images courtesy of guinnessworldrecords.com. These images are for information only, are significant to the article and are reproduced under fair use terms. The images are rendered in low resolution to avoid piracy. It is believed these images will not in any way limit the ability of the copyright owners to market or sell their product.
Page 50 – Bell magazine advertisement, 1950s. Source unknown. Pre-1978, no copyright renewal (PD image).
Page 51 – Lewis, source: en.wikipedia.org/wiki/Jerry_Lee_Lewis. Pre-1978, no copyright mark (PD image). – Haley, source: commons.wikimedia.org/wiki/Category:Bill_Haley_%26_His_Comets. Pre-1978, no copyright mark (PD image). – Sun Records, source: commons.wikimedia.org/wiki/File:Sun_Studio,_Memphis.jpg. Pre-1978, no copyright mark (PD image).
Page 52 – Prado, source: granma.cu/cultura/2017-11-17/mambo-que-rico-es-17-11-2017-22-11-42 creator unknown. – Haley, sheet music cover image from *Rock Around the Clock*, Decca Records. Source: wikiwand.com/en/ Rock_Around_the_Clock. – Boone, source: en.wikipedia.org/wiki/Pat_Boone. – Gibbs, record cover of *Dance With Me Henry* for Modern Records 1955. All images this page Pre-1978, no copyright renewal (PD images).
Page 53 – Sinatra by Columbia Pictures 1957, source: en.wikipedia.org/wiki/Frank_Sinatra. Pre-1978, (PD image). – Cole publicity photo by GAC 1958, source: commons.wikimedia.org/wiki/File:Nat_King_Cole_1958.JPG. Pre-1978, (PD image).
Page 54 – Dress, 1955. Source: flickr.com/photos/30453277@N03/6526062925. Pre-1978, no mark (PD image).
Page 55 – From Vogue Magazine, Summer 1955. Source: eBay.com (PD image).*
Page 56 – Fashion magazine covers from 1955. Pre 1978, no copyright mark (PD image).*
Page 57 – Bellas Hess Catalog, Spring-Summer 1955, (PD image).*

Page 58 – From *Life* Mag, 7th Nov 1955. Source: books.google.com/books?id=xFQEAAAAMBAJ&printsec (PD image).*
Page 59 – From Vanity Fair, May 1953. Source: likesoldclothes.tumblr.com/tagged/1953/ (PD image).*
Page 60 – Celebrity advert from Life Magazine 1st Jun 1953. Source: books.google.com.sg/books?id=30cEAAAAMBAJ&printsec (PD image).* – Haslam Dresscutting patterns, Summer No.31, 1954. Pre 1978 (PD image).*
Page 61 – From *Life* Mag, 4th July 1955. Source: books.google.com/books?id=r1YEAAAAMBAJ&printsec. (PD image).*
Page 62 – Marilyn Monroe in 1952 studio publicity portrait for film Niagara, by 20th Century Fox. (PD image). – Models walking photo. Source: Jessica at myvintagevogue.com. Licensed under CC BY 2.0.
Page 63 – Sinatra, source: morrisonhotelgallery.com/collections/wtvp8g/The-Sinatra-Experience-.
– Brando, source: dailybreak.co/wp-content/uploads/2019/06/Marlon-Brando-Ford-Thunderbird-1955-Est.-2444.jpg.
– Dean, source: en.wikipedia.org/wiki/James_Dean. All images this page Pre-1978, no copyright mark (PD image).
Page 64 – Source: blog.hola.com/hongkongblues/2017/03/rosa-ahumado. Pre-1978, no copyright mark (PD image).
Page 65 – From *Life* mag, 7th Mar 1955. Source: books.google.com/books?id=JFQEAAAAMBAJ&printsec. (PD image).*
Page 66 – Young girl, source: polioplace.org/history/artifacts/reluctant-poster-child. Pre-1978, no mark (PD image).
– Iron Lung ward, source: commons.wikimedia.org/wiki/File:Iron_Lung_ward-Rancho_Los_Amigos_Hospital.gif by fda.gov (PD image). – Children's ward, source: imgur.com/gallery/vdwfM40. Pre-1978, no copyright mark (PD image).
Page 67 – GAM-63 RASCAL, source: commons.wikimedia.org/wiki/File:GAM-63_RASCAL_on_trailer.jpg from the U.S. Air Force (PD image). – *Oklahoma!* film poster, 1955 by RKO Radio Pictures.**
Source: en.wikipedia.org/wiki/Oklahoma!_(1955_film).
Page 68 – Coke advertisement, source unknown. Pre-1978, no copyright mark (PD image).* – USS Nautilus (SSN 571), 21st Jan 1954, from U.S. Navy. Source: commons.wikimedia.org/wiki/File:Nautiluscore.jpg. (PD image).
Page 69 – Le Manns 1955, creator unknown. Source: carlosghys.be/html/biography_luc.html. Pre-1978, no copyright mark (PD image). – *Lolita* book cover, 1955, by Vladimir Nabokov.** (PD image). – *Lolita* movie poster, 1962, by MGM.** Source: en.wikipedia.org/wiki/Lolita_(1962_film)#/media/File:Lolita_(1962_film_poster).jpg.
Page 70 – From *Life* mag, 7th Mar 1955. Source: books.google.com/books?id=JFQEAAAAMBAJ&printsec. (PD image).*
Page 71 – From *Life* mag, 3rd Jan 1965. Source: books.google.com/books?id=_VMEAAAAMBAJ&printsec. (PD image).*
Page 72-74 – All photos are, where possible, CC BY 2.0 or PD images made available by the creator for free use including commercial use. Where commercial use photos are unavailable, photos are included here for information only under U.S. fair use laws due to: 1- images are low resolution copies; 2- images do not devalue the ability of the copyright holders to profit from the original works in any way; 3- Images are too small to be used to make illegal copies for use in another book; 4- The images are relevant to the article created.
Page 75 – From *Life* Mag, 1st Aug 1955. Source: books.google.com/books?id=xIYEAAAAMBAJ&printsec. (PD image).*
Page 78 – From *Life* Mag, 7th Mar 1955. Source: books.google.com/books?id=JFQEAAAAMBAJ&printsec. (PD image).*
Page 79 – Greyhound print magazine advertisement, source: eBay (PD image).*

*Advertisement (or image from an advertisement) is in the public domain because it was published in a collective work (such as a periodical issue) in the US between 1925 and 1977 and without a copyright notice specific to the advertisement.
**Posters for movies or events are either in the public domain (published in the US between 1925 and 1977 and without a copyright notice specific to the artwork) or owned by the production company, creator, or distributor of the movie or event. Posters, where not in the public domain, and screen stills from movies or TV shows, are reproduced here under USA Fair Use laws due to: 1- images are low resolution copies; 2- images do not devalue the ability of the copyright holders to profit from the original works in any way; 3- Images are too small to be used to make illegal copies for use in another book; 4- The images are relevant to the article created.

This book was written by Bernard Bradforsand-Tyler as part of *A Time Traveler's Guide* series of books.

All rights reserved. The author exerts the moral right to be identified as the author of the work.

No parts of this book may be reproduced, stored in any retrieval system, or transmitted in any form or by any means, without prior written permission from the author.

This is a work of nonfiction. No names have been changed, no events have been fabricated. The content of this book is provided as a source of information for the reader, however it is not meant as a substitute for direct expert opinion. Although the author has made every effort to ensure that the information in this book is correct at time of printing, and while this publication is designed to provide accurate information in regard to the subject matters covered, the author assumes no responsibility for errors, inaccuracies, omissions, or any other inconsistencies herein and hereby disclaims any liability to any party for any loss, damage, or disruption caused by errors or omissions.

All images contained herein are reproduced with the following permissions:
- Images included in the public domain.
- Images obtained under creative commons license.
- Images included under fair use terms.
- Images reproduced with owner's permission.

All image attributions and source credits are provided at the back of the book. All images are the property of their respective owners and are protected under international copyright laws.

First printed in 2020 in the USA (ISBN 979-8684074448).
2nd Ed 2021 (978-0645062328), 3rd Ed 2024 (978-1922676313).
Self-published by B. Bradforsand-Tyler.

www.ingramcontent.com/pod-product-compliance
Lightning Source LLC
Chambersburg PA
CBHW072104110526
44590CB00018B/3310